To Eat Or Not To Eat?

The Fruits Group – Food Pyramid

(2nd Grade Science Series)

SPEEDY
PUBLISHING

Speedy Publishing LLC
40 E. Main St. #1156
Newark, DE 19711
www.speedypublishing.com

Fruits are the sweet-tasting seed-bearing parts of plants, or occasionally sweet parts of plants which do not bear seeds.

Fruits are low in calories and fat and are a source of natural sugars, fiber and vitamins.

Processing fruits when canning or making into juices may add sugars and remove nutrients.

The fruit food group is sometimes combined with the vegetable food group.

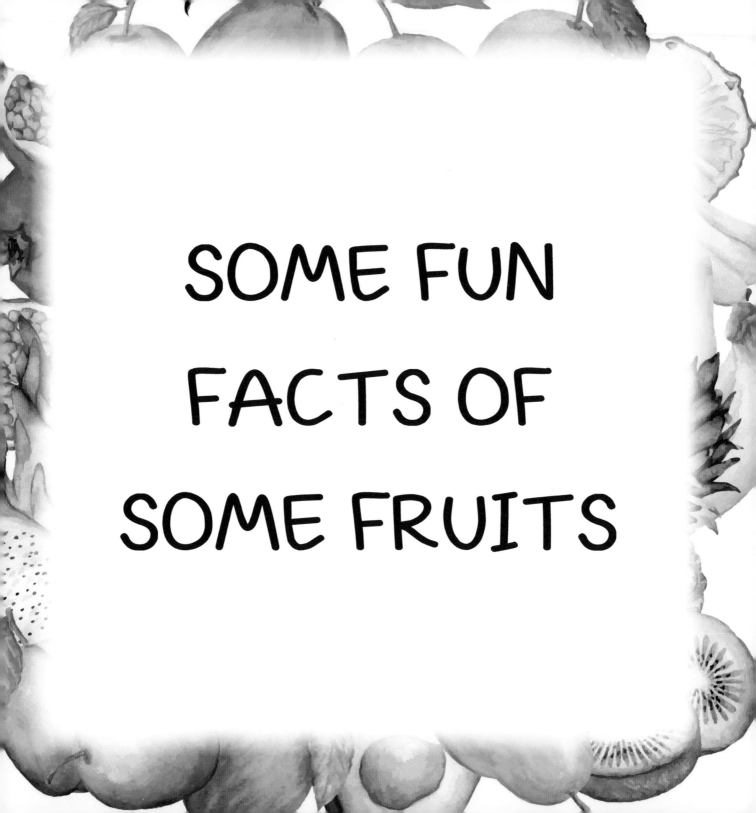

SOME FUN FACTS OF SOME FRUITS

A strawberry is
not an actual berry,
but a banana is.

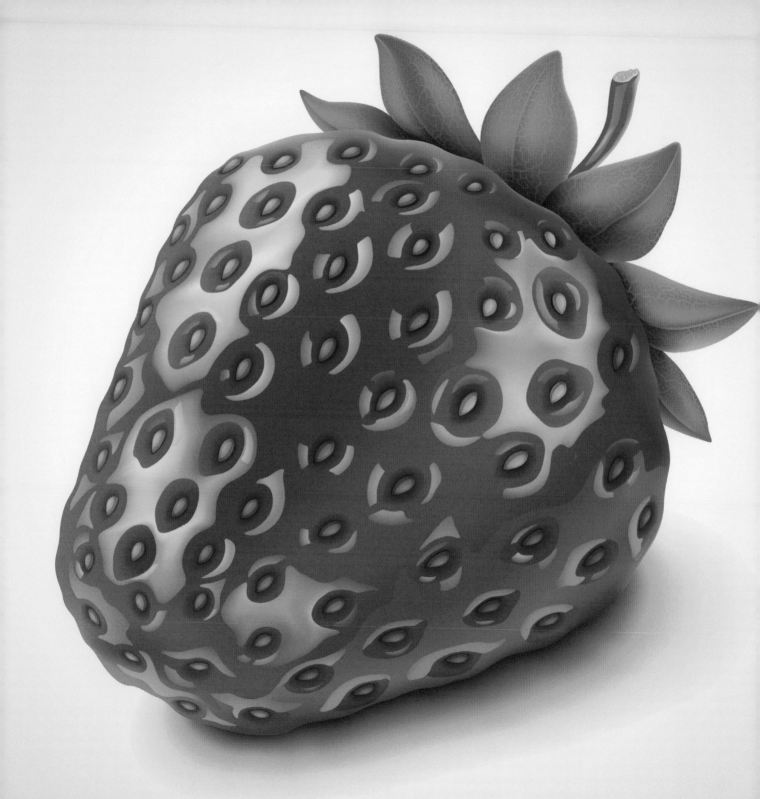

Apples float in water because they are twenty-five percent air.

Tomatoes are a fruit not a vegetable. Tomatoes are the most popular fruits in the world.

Bananas have a natural antacid effect in the body, so if you suffer from heartburn, try eating a banana for soothing relief.

An average strawberry
has around two
hundred seeds.

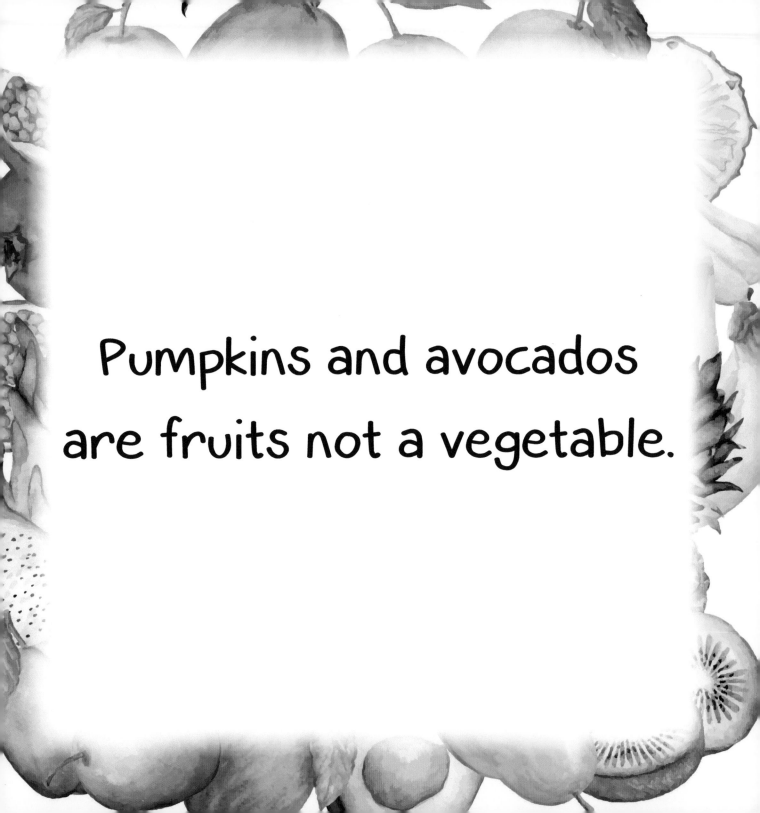

Pumpkins and avocados are fruits not a vegetable.

Dark green vegetables include more vitamin C than light green color vegetables.

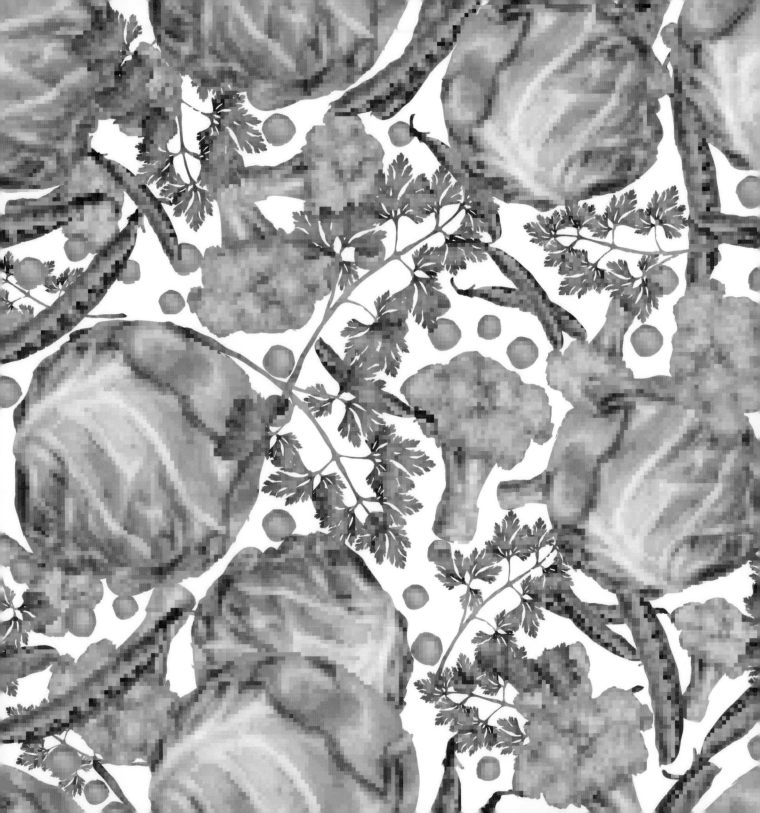

Because bananas are easy to digest and are very nutritious they are the first fruit offered to babies.

An apple tree can produce up to four hundred apples a year.

COLOR THE FRUITS

Printed in Great Britain
by Amazon

39217859R00021